RESCUE RIDERS

COAST GUARD BOATS TO THE RESCUE!

I0811291

BY FRANCES NAGLE

Gareth Stevens PUBLISHING

Please visit our website, www.garethstevens.com. For a free color catalog of all our high-quality books, call toll free 1-800-542-2595 or fax 1-877-542-2596.

Library of Congress Cataloging-in-Publication Data
Names: Nagle, Frances, author.
Title: Coast Guard boats to the rescue! / Frances Nagle.
Description: New York : Gareth Stevens Publishing, [2023] | Series: Rescue riders | Includes index.
Identifiers: LCCN 2021046624 (print) | LCCN 2021046625 (ebook) | ISBN 9781538278482 (set) | ISBN 9781538278499 (library binding) | ISBN 9781538278475 (paperback) | ISBN 9781538278505 (ebook)
Subjects: LCSH: United States. Coast Guard–Juvenile literature. | Search and rescue operations–Juvenile literature. | Government vessels–United States–Juvenile literature.
Classification: LCC VG53 .N34 2023 (print) | LCC VG53 (ebook) | DDC 363.28/60973–dc23
LC record available at https://lccn.loc.gov/2021046624
LC ebook record available at https://lccn.loc.gov/2021046625

Published in 2023 by
Gareth Stevens Publishing
29 E. 21st Street
New York, NY 10010

Portions of this work were originally authored by B. J. Best and published as *Coast Guard Boats*. All new material this edition authored by Frances Nagle.

Copyright © 2023 Gareth Stevens Publishing

Designer: Leslie Taylor
Editor: Kristen Nelson

Photo credits: Cover photoff/Shutterstock.com; pp. 2-24 (background texture) Pixel Embargo/Shutterstock.com; p. 5 muratart/Shutterstock.com; p. 7 https://commons.wikimedia.org/wiki/File:U.S._naval_forces_maintain_presence_of_Cape_Verde_DVIDS202836.jpg; p. 9 Photo_Time/Shutterstock.com; p. 11 Stock-Asso/Shutterstock.com; p. 13 Photo courtesy of the U.S. Coast Guard/https://www.uscg.mil/Assets/Display/Article/1825014/47-foot-motor-life-boat/; p. 15 (inset) https://commons.wikimedia.org/wiki/File:Coast_Guard_Cutter_Sledge_sets_buoy_in_Potomac_River.jpg; p. 15 https://commons.wikimedia.org/wiki/File:Air-boat_operations_in_Bayou_La_Batre,_Ala._DVIDS1107510.jpg; p. 17 Photo courtesy of the U.S. Coast Guard/https://www.uscg.mil/Assets/Display/Article/1816423/national-security-cutter/; p. 19 https://commons.wikimedia.org/wiki/File:Unexpected_Visitor_(16667486340).jpg; p. 21 ArnoudNL/Shutterstock.com.

All rights reserved. No part of this book may be reproduced in any form without permission in writing from the publisher, except by a reviewer.

Printed in the United States of America

CPSIA compliance information: Batch #CSGS23: For further information contact Gareth Stevens, New York, New York at 1-800-542-2595.

Find us on

CONTENTS

Boldface words appear in the glossary.

Call the Coast Guard!

A boat has stopped working while out fishing on the ocean. The waves are pushing it farther from shore. Luckily, the passengers can call the U.S. Coast Guard! U.S. Coast Guard boats go out when there are **emergencies** on the water.

On the Job

The U.S. Coast Guard keeps **ports** safe. It makes sure laws are followed. It also helps boats that have been **damaged** or are in need of other kinds of aid. Coastguardsmen are often the first to respond to problems on the water.

U.S. COAST GUARD

The coast guard works in the lakes and rivers of the United States and off the country's coast. The coast is where the sea meets the land. Thousands of people in the coast guard work on the boats in the coast guard's **fleet**.

6595
U.S. COAST GUARD
U.S. COAST GUARD

Radio in an Emergency

People on boats in need of help often use a **radio** to call the coast guard. They tell what the emergency is. The coast guard sends a boat to help. Coastguardsmen move fast when there's a fire, **medical** emergency, or boat that has **capsized**.

FAV
TAG
16
CH
SCAN
DUAL

Boats on the Way

The coast guard uses many boats. Some are specially made for finding people and boats in trouble. The 47-foot (14 m) motor lifeboat is used in bad weather. It's made for when the conditions in the water are the worst.

U.S. COAST GUARD
47260

Some boats work with buoys. Buoys are floating objects that show other boats where to go. An airboat has a fan on the back. It can go places other boats can't. It can even go down flooded streets!

coast guard buoy

Cutters

The coast guard uses big boats on the ocean. A cutter is a boat longer than 65 feet (20 m). Coastguardsmen can live on them. Some cutters carry other coast guard boats on them. They may carry helicopters too!

U.S. COAST GUARD
750

Icebreakers

Some coast guard boats do special things. An icebreaker smashes ice so other boats can travel through icy water. One, the *Polar Star*, works in the Arctic. Other icebreakers work on the **Great Lakes**. They help **cargo** ships move through the lakes in winter.

Polar Star

Help on the Water

Some people call the coast guard with an emergency. Others may just need a tow to shore. Coast guard boats are as important on water as ambulances and fire trucks are on land. They help keep people safe!

RS05
RS05
WESTKAPELLE
KNRM
SAR

GLOSSARY

capsize: to turn over so the bottom is on top

cargo: goods carried by a plane, train, or truck

damage: to harm

emergency: an unexpected situation that needs quick action

fleet: a group of ships

Great Lakes: the five lakes found on or near the border of the United States and Canada

medical: having to do with care given by doctors

port: a town or city where ships stop to load and unload cargo

radio: a device that is used to send and receive messages by radio